CHATGPT FOR LANGUAGE TEACHERS

The Ultimate Prompt Handbook for AI Productivity

David Weller

Book Cover by David Weller

First edition, May 2023

CONTENTS

Introduction 1

Privacy 2

Transparency 3

Plagiarism & Ethics 4

Bias 5

How to Use This Book 6

Lesson Planning 7

- Lesson Plan Aims 8
- Lesson Context 9
- Brainstorming Activities 10
- Lesson Plan 11
- Use a Lesson Plan to Train ChatGPT 12
- Editing Lesson Plans 13
- Lesson Plan Feedback 14
- Lesson Methodologies 15
- Competition and Collaboration 16
- Language Examples 17
- Language Explanations 18
- Task Differentiation 19
- Understanding L1 & Culture 20
- Writing IPA 21

Worksheets & Materials 23

- Anagrams 24

Debate Cards 25
Dialogues 26
Gap Fills / Cloze Activities 27
Gap Fill / Cloze Stories 28
Jigsaw Reading 29
Jumbled Sentences 30
Mad Libs 31
Match Words & Definitions 32
Multiple Choice Quiz 33
Reading & Listening Comprehension 34
Roleplay Cards 35
Storytelling Prompts 36
Surveys & Questionnaires 37
Tongue Twisters 38
True or False 39
Wordsearch 40
In The Classroom 41
Graded Language 42
Classroom Management 43
Giving Instructions 44
Concept-Checking Questions 45
Errors & Feedback 46
Assessment & Grading 47
Formative Assessment 48
Student Self-Assessment 49

Summative Assessment 50
Written Feedback 51
Create a Rubric 52
Grade with a Rubric 53
Professional Development 55
Ask Questions 56
Summarizing 57
Research Questions 58
Admin & Data 59
Write Reports 60
Write & Summarize Emails 61
Final Words 63
The Future 64
Other Books by the Author 65

INTRODUCTION

Welcome to the world of using AI for language teaching!

With AI rapidly improving, it's transforming the way that students learn, and teachers teach. AI is probably going to be the biggest affect on education since the internet itself (whether it's even bigger, only time will tell).

Right now, we're in the earliest stages of AI, and one of the most advanced tools currently is ChatGPT.

I hope that this book will give you a quick, easy guide to mastering this tool for you and your students. It will do this by helping you with prompts (the instructions you type into it) and plugins to expand its capability.

The sections are divided by the type of task that we teachers use the most. The sections are:

- Lesson planning
- In the classroom
- Assessment and grading
- Professional development
- Admin and data

They should be self-explanatory, but the contents list earlier should help you jump to the specific prompts you need most.

As AI tools advance, I'll update this book periodically, so check back occasionally.

Good luck with your teaching!

David Weller (the barefootTEFLteacher)

PRIVACY

By default, ChatGPT collects your data and uses it for training purposes.

You can opt-out of this by clicking or tapping on your name, going to settings, data controls, and toggling the switch labelled 'Chat History & Training' to the off position.

Like this:

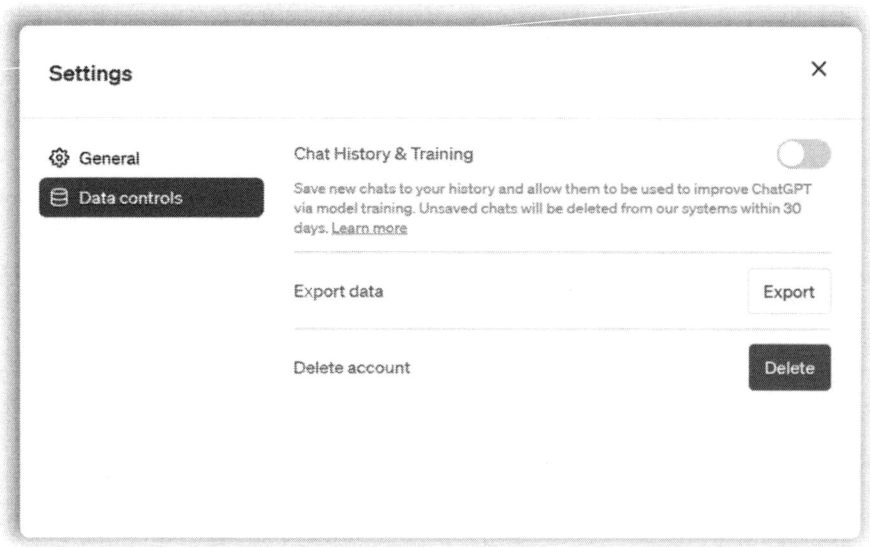

TRANSPARENCY

While it's up to you, I would suggest letting people know when you've used AI to help you create something.

For example, I used ChatGPT to fine-tune some of the prompts in this book, but I didn't just copy-and-paste.

Here's why transparency matters:

Builds Trust: By being honest about your use of AI, you create an environment of trust and openness with others.

Encourages Ethical Use: It helps set the standard for how technology should be used, ensuring that we consider its impact on society and the people around us.

Mitigates Misunderstandings: When others are aware that you're using AI, it can prevent potential misunderstandings or misinterpretations.

Promotes Accountability: Being transparent about AI usage encourages a culture of accountability. It helps you acknowledge the limitations of AI and take responsibility for its output.

Reduces the Stigma: By being open about using AI, you help reduce the stigma associated with seeking assistance from technology.

Sets an example: Your actions model good practice for colleagues and students.

Embrace the power of AI, but always remember to use it responsibly and transparently.

PLAGIARISM & ETHICS

While it might be tempting to use pretend AI output is your own work, it can backfire.

Detection software is always evolving to keep pace with new AI models, so copy-pasting AI content will be harder to do undetected. Why would you risk your reputation or even career?

You won't develop your own style, or voice, if you rely too much on AI content. You'll rob yourself of your ability to develop and grow.

You can use AI generated content as a starting point for your own work, or even as a proof-reader of finished work. Used this way, it becomes a tool for efficiency and growth, not of plagiarism.

On a final note, this applies to your students as well. Take time to teach them the implications of AI so they don't fall into the plagiarism trap.

BIAS

AI can have biases built in, intentionally or unintentionally.

It's on you to ensure that whatever you create accurately reflects what you want it to.

As with any source that you read, take your time to critically assess it, and report it if it seems 'off'.

In ChatGPT you can do this by clicking or tapping the 'thumbs down' icon next to the output text, and you'll be able to report it via a form that looks like this:

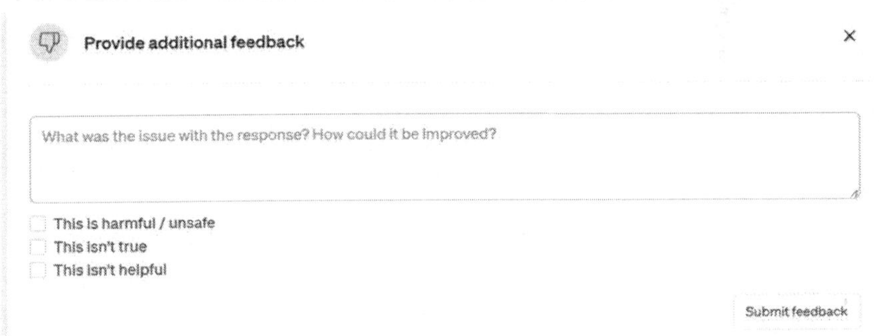

HOW TO USE THIS BOOK

Page Layout

Each topic has two sections; 'prompt' and 'examples'

The 'prompt' section is a prompt template, that you'll need to edit before you use. The information in [brackets] is meant to be replaced with information that's appropriate for you and your teaching context.

The 'examples' section has some examples of what this might look like for different age groups, language levels, and types of lesson.

Which version of ChatGPT?

All the prompts were tested on ChatGPT v4, (March 23, 2023 version) and have given good results.

Remember to always experiment to get the best results.

Be creative!

Think of each prompt as a starting point. You can add information, take it away, or ask ChatGPT to edit the result that it gives you.

Take time to experiment and record your best prompts for later.

Have fun!

LESSON PLANNING

LESSON PLAN AIMS

PROMPT

"Please create a gap-fill activity using this [insert vocabulary, grammar or pronunciation focus] in the form of a short story.

Please use the [vocabulary / grammar / specific sound] as the gap.

Please use [beginner] level English."

EXAMPLES

"Please create a gap-fill activity using common zoo animals.

Please use the animal names as the gap.

Please use beginner level English."

"Please create a gap-fill activity using present perfect tense sentences.

Please use the verbs as the gap.

Please use intermediate level English."

LESSON CONTEXT

PROMPT

"Please give me suggestions for a good context for my ESL lesson.

I need to teach [language focus], but want a [descriptive] context that my [type of] students will enjoy.

They enjoy [what your students find interesting]"

EXAMPLES

"Please give me suggestions for a good context for my ESL lesson.

I need to teach the past simple, but want a fun, imaginary context that my young students will enjoy.

They enjoy sports and superheroes"

"Please give me suggestions for a good context for my ESL lesson.

I need a realistic context for my business English students to practice business idioms in a conversation."

They enjoy whole class discussions and pairwork.

BRAINSTORMING ACTIVITIES

PROMPT

"Please brainstorm a list of five engaging classroom activities that promote the development of [language skill or focus] in students.

Provide a brief description of each activity, the target language proficiency level, and the learning objectives it addresses.

Include any necessary materials, resources, or technology that would enhance the effectiveness of these activities in a language-learning environment."

EXAMPLES

"Please brainstorm a list of five engaging classroom activities that promote the development of listening in students.

Provide a brief description of each activity, the target language proficiency level, and the learning objectives it addresses.

Include any necessary materials, resources, or technology that would enhance the effectiveness of these activities in a language-learning environment."

LESSON PLAN

PROMPT

"Please help me write a TEFL lesson plan.

Lesson aim: by the end of the lesson, students should be better able to [lesson aim].

Students: Age: [age range]. Level: [English level]

Class length: [time]

Context: [language learning context]

Methodology: [teaching methodology]"

EXAMPLE

"Please help me write a TEFL lesson plan.

Lesson aim: by the end of the lesson, students should be better able to use 'can/can't' to describe action verbs.

Students: 7-9 years old, beginner level (A1/A2 on CEFR)

Class length: 60 minutes

Context: visiting a zoo and describing what the animals are doing.

Methodology: Engage-Study-Activate (ESA)"

USE A LESSON PLAN TO TRAIN CHATGPT

PROMPT

"I would like you to write a TEFL lesson plan in the style of a lesson plan I will give you.

Lesson aim: by the end of the lesson, students should be better able to [lesson aim].

Students: Age: [age range].

Level: [English level]

Class length: [time]

Context: [language learning context]

Methodology: [teaching methodology]"

Here's the lesson plan you should use as inspiration:

[paste a previous lesson plan]

Please generate a lesson plan in using my aim, in the style of the lesson plan example I gave you."

EDITING LESSON PLANS

PROMPT

"Please edit the lesson plan you've just generated. [describe the change you'd like to make]".

EXAMPLES

"Please edit the lesson plan you've just generated. Put it in a table"

"Please edit the lesson plan you've just generated. Add a warmer activity at the beginning but keep the whole lesson plan at 60 minutes long".

"Please edit the lesson plan you've just generated. Change the methodology to be Task-Based Learning".

"Please edit the lesson plan you've just generated. Add a pairwork discussion activity after the vocabulary is introduced, so the students can practice the new vocabulary they've just learned".

LESSON PLAN FEEDBACK

PROMPT

"Here's my lesson plan. Please give me feedback on how I can improve it. Please consider all aspects of teaching and learning theory. Please focus on [area] in particular.

Any and all feedback is welcome. [Paste your lesson plan here]".

EXAMPLE

"Here's my lesson plan. Please give me feedback on how I can improve it. Please consider all aspects of teaching and learning theory. Please focus on lesson staging in particular.

Any and all feedback is welcome.

[Paste your lesson plan here]".

LESSON METHODOLOGIES

PROMPT

"Revise a lesson plan that currently follows [Methodology 1] and transform it into [methodology 2].

Identify the original lesson's objective, target language, and main activities, and then develop a new sequence of tasks that promote student-centred, meaningful language use in context.

Ensure that the lesson maintains its original learning objectives while offering increased opportunities for student interaction and authentic communication."

EXAMPLES

"Revise a lesson plan that currently follows the [Presentation, Practice, and Production (PPP) methodology and transform it into a Task-Based Learning (TBL) approach.

Identify the original lesson's objective, target language, and main activities, and then develop a new sequence of tasks that promote student-centred, meaningful language use in context.

Ensure that the lesson maintains its original learning objectives while offering increased opportunities for student interaction and authentic communication."

COMPETITION AND COLLABORATION

PROMPT

"Please change a language teaching activity that is [competitive/collaborative] into one that is [competitive/collaborative].

Identify the original activity's objective and target language and then change the activity as instructed, keeping the objective and target language the same.

Here is the activity: [paste activity]"

EXAMPLES

"Please change a language teaching activity that is competitive into one that is collaborative.

Identify the original activity's objective and target language and then change the activity as instructed, keeping the objective and target language the same.

Here is the activity: [paste activity]"

LANGUAGE EXAMPLES

PROMPT

"Develop a focused language activity that helps students explore the use of [language focus].

Design a context, (or use [this context]) and include example sentences showcasing [language focus] along with appropriate usage in the given context."

EXAMPLES

"Develop a focused language activity that helps students explore the use of modal verbs for expressing possibility, necessity, and permission.

Design a context, and include example sentences showcasing different modal verbs (e.g., can, could, must, should) along with their appropriate usage in the given context."

"Develop a focused language activity that helps students explore the use of [vocabulary related to holiday travel].

The context is 'travelling for a holiday' , please include example sentences showcasing new words along with appropriate usage in the given context."

LANGUAGE EXPLANATIONS

PROMPT

I'm a language teacher and want to give my students a language explanation.

Prepare a concise and clear explanation of [language point], along with examples to illustrate this in context. Then, create a step-by-step guide for me on how to present this in a way that enhances my students' understanding and helps them avoid common mistakes.

EXAMPLES

"I'm a language teacher and want to give my students a language explanation.

Prepare a concise and clear explanation of the present perfect vs the past simple, along with examples to illustrate this in context. Then, create a step-by-step guide for me on how to present this in a way that enhances my students' understanding and helps them avoid common mistakes."

TASK DIFFERENTIATION

PROMPT

"Please create a language teaching [type of activity] around the theme 'A Day in the Life of a Superhero' with [number] distinct difficulty levels: [competency levels]

Adapt the linguistic complexity, range of vocabulary, and the required level of skill and creativity in each task to suit the target proficiency level."

EXAMPLES

"Design three versions of a language teaching conversation task on the topic of planning a weekend trip, catering to three different proficiency levels: beginner, intermediate, and advanced.

Adapt the linguistic complexity, range of vocabulary, and the required level of skill and creativity in each task to suit the target proficiency level."

"Create a language teaching storytelling activity around the theme 'A Day in the Life of a Superhero' with three distinct difficulty levels: elementary, pre-intermediate, and upper-intermediate.

Adapt the linguistic complexity, range of vocabulary, and the required level of skill and creativity in each task to suit the target proficiency level."

UNDERSTANDING L1 & CULTURE

PROMPT

“My students’ first language (L1) is/are [language(s)]. I want to understand any unique linguistic features or challenges it may present when they learn English.

Please create a brief report to analyse how this L1’s grammatical structures, vocabulary, and pronunciation patterns might influence my students' English language learning.

Include recommendations for teaching strategies or activities that specifically address these L1 influences to facilitate a more effective language learning experience."

EXAMPLES

“My students’ first language (L1) is/are [Chinese]. I want to understand any unique linguistic features or challenges it may present when they learn English.

Please create a brief report to analyse how this L1’s grammatical structures, vocabulary, and pronunciation patterns might influence my students' English language learning.

Include recommendations for teaching strategies or activities that specifically address these L1 influences to facilitate a more effective language learning experience."

WRITING IPA

PROMPT

"Select [number] English accents, such as [accents].

Choose a common sentence or short phrase and transcribe it using the International Phonetic Alphabet (IPA) for each accent.

Explain the key differences in pronunciation, including vowel and consonant sounds, that contribute to the distinct characteristics of each accent.

Additionally, provide tips for teachers on how to guide students in practicing these accents and improving their pronunciation skills."

EXAMPLES

"Select three English accents, such as General American, Received Pronunciation (British), and Australian English.

Choose a common sentence or short phrase and transcribe it using the International Phonetic Alphabet (IPA) for each accent.

Explain the key differences in pronunciation, including vowel and consonant sounds, that contribute to the distinct characteristics of each accent.

Additionally, provide tips for teachers on how to guide students in practicing these accents and improving their pronunciation skills."

WORKSHEETS & MATERIALS

ANAGRAMS

PROMPT

"Please create an anagram puzzle for me in a codeblock. Underneath please tell me the solutions. Here are the words to use to create the puzzle: [10-15 words]."

EXAMPLE

"Please create an anagram puzzle for me in a codeblock. Underneath please tell me the solutions. Here are the words to use to create the puzzle: [10-15 words]."

Jaguar Leopard Sloth Chimpanzee Tiger Crocodile Elephant Gorilla Monkey Lion Tiger

[Please note that this prompt only works in ChatGPT version 3]

DEBATE CARDS

PROMPT

"Create debate role cards for language students to engage in a debate about the [topic].

Each card should represent a different perspective, and include a brief description of the viewpoint, key arguments to support their stance, and potential counterarguments to address.

Please keep the language level [level]."

EXAMPLE

"Create debate role cards for students to engage in a debate about the impact of video games on society.

Each card should represent a different perspective, and include a brief description of the viewpoint, key arguments to support their stance, and potential counterarguments to address."

Please keep the language level to pre-intermediate level."

DIALOGUES

PROMPT

"Create a dialogue for language students to practice their comprehension skills, focusing on the topic of [topic]. Please include [number] characters in the dialogue".

The students are [level] language students, so please create it at this level.

The dialogue should be engaging, informative, and funny if possible."

EXAMPLE

"Create a dialogue for language students to practice their comprehension skills, focusing on the topic of requesting a refund from a rude customer service staff. Please include three characters in the dialogue".

The students are pre-intermediate language students, so please create it at this level.

The dialogue should be engaging, informative, and funny if possible."

GAP FILLS / CLOZE ACTIVITIES

PROMPT

"Please create a gap-fill activity using this [insert vocabulary, grammar or pronunciation sound].

Please use the [vocabulary / grammar / sound] as the gap.

Please use [beginner] level English."

EXAMPLES

"Please create a gap-fill activity using common zoo animals.

Please use the animal names as the gap.

Please use beginner level English."

"Please create a gap-fill activity using present perfect tense sentences.

Please use the verbs as the gap.

Please use intermediate level English."

"Please create a gap-fill activity with words that have the sounds / θ/ or /s/

Please only use the words that have those sounds as the gap.

Please use beginner level English."

GAP FILL / CLOZE STORIES

PROMPT

"Please create a gap-fill activity using this [insert vocabulary, grammar or pronunciation sound] in the form of a short story.

Please use the [vocabulary / grammar] as the gap.

Please use [beginner] level English."

EXAMPLES

"Please create a gap-fill activity using common zoo animals.

Please use the animal names as the gap.

Please use beginner level English."

"Please create a gap-fill activity using present perfect tense sentences.

Please use the verbs as the gap.

Please use intermediate level English."

"Please create a gap-fill activity with words that have the sounds /th/ or /s/

Please only use the words that have those sounds as the gap.

Please use beginner level English."

JIGSAW READING

PROMPT

"Please generate a jigsaw reading text.

It should be a short story about [number] of people who [saw or did an activity]

There should be [same number] of versions. Each version should be from a different character's point of view and have different information.

Each student will receive a version. The students should read their version, then discuss with each other, in order to work out what really happened. Please include an answer key."

EXAMPLE

"Please generate a jigsaw reading text.

It should be a short story about three people who saw a crime.

There should be three versions. Each version should be from a different character's point of view and have different information.

Each student will receive a version. The students should read their version, then discuss with each other, in order to work out what really happened. Please include an answer key."

JUMBLED SENTENCES

PROMPT

"Please create a jumbled sentence puzzle for me.

Here are the sentences to use to create the puzzle: [sentences].

Please include an answer key."

EXAMPLE

"Please create a jumbled sentence puzzle for me.

Here are the sentences to use to create the puzzle:

1. The cat is sitting on the mat.
2. The dog is eating food.
3. The fox is sleeping in the garden.

Please include an answer key."

MAD LIBS

PROMPT

"Create a mad libs story activity for students to practice their creative writing skills and vocabulary related to the topic of [topic].

The mad libs story should include blank spaces for students to fill in with appropriate words such as [word types].

Provide a list of suggested words for each blank space and an example of how the completed story might look."

EXAMPLE

"Create a mad libs story activity for students to practice their creative writing skills and vocabulary related to the topic of 'A Day at the Zoo'.

The mad libs story should include blank spaces for students to fill in with appropriate words such as nouns, verbs, adjectives, and adverbs.

Provide a list of suggested words for each blank space and an example of how the completed story might look."

MATCH WORDS & DEFINITIONS

PROMPT

"Generate a word-matching activity for language learners. I'll give you a list of words.

Please create a table with the words and definitions that need to be matched.

Here's the list of words to use: [list of words]".

EXAMPLE

"Generate a word-matching activity for language learners. I'll give you a list of words.

Please create a table with the words and definitions that need to be matched.

Here's the list of words to use:

Destination, Accommodation, Itinerary, Souvenir, Passport, Ticket, Luggage, Tourist, Guidebook, Transportation"

MULTIPLE CHOICE QUIZ

PROMPT

"Please generate a multiple-choice quiz for language learners. The topic is [topic]. There should be [number] questions.

Please include these words or information to quiz on: [specific knowledge].

Please include an answer key."

EXAMPLE

"Please generate a multiple-choice quiz for language learners. The topic is holidays. There should be 10 questions.

Please include these words or information to quiz on:

The capital of China is Beijing; The definition of 'passport'; The definition of 'souvenir'; the difference between present perfect and past simple'.

Please include an answer key."

READING & LISTENING COMPREHENSION

PROMPT

"Create a reading text or listening script for language students to practice their comprehension skills, focusing on the topic of [topic]. The students are [level] language students, so please create it at this level.

The text or script should be engaging, informative, and include various aspects of [topic] such as its benefits, challenges, and common misconceptions.

After the text or script, provide a set of comprehension questions to test the students' understanding of the topic. Please include a suggested answer key."

EXAMPLE

"Create a reading text or listening script for students to practice their comprehension skills, focusing on the topic of recycling.

The students are intermediate level language students, so please create it at this level.

The text or script should be engaging, informative, and include various aspects of recycling, such as its benefits, challenges, and common misconceptions.

After the text or script, provide a set of comprehension questions to test the students' understanding of the topic. Please include a suggested answer key."

ROLEPLAY CARDS

PROMPT

"Create role-play cards for language students to engage in a conversation about the [topic].

Each card should represent a different perspective, and include a brief description of the viewpoint, possible opinions, and questions to ask during the discussion."

Please keep the language level [level]."

EXAMPLE

"Create role-play cards for students to engage in a conversation about the benefits and challenges of social media.

Each card should represent a different perspective, and include a brief description of the viewpoint, possible opinions, and questions to ask during the discussion."

Please keep the language level to pre-intermediate level."

STORYTELLING PROMPTS

PROMPT

"Generate a list of [number] imaginative storytelling writing prompts for language students to use as a starting point for their creative writing.

Each prompt should include an interesting scenario, character, or setting that encourages students to explore their creativity and develop a unique story.

The topic for all prompts should be [topic].

The level of the students is [student level], and their writing should focus on [language point]".

EXAMPLE

"Generate a list of 5 imaginative storytelling writing prompts for language students to use as a starting point for their creative writing.

Each prompt should include an interesting scenario, character, or setting that encourages students to explore their creativity and develop a unique story.

The topic for all prompts should be superheroes.

The level of the students is pre-intermediate, and their writing should focus on using the past progressive tense".

SURVEYS & QUESTIONNAIRES

PROMPT

"Create a survey for students to gather opinions and experiences about [topic] from their fellow students.

The survey should include [number] questions of a variety of open-ended and multiple-choice questions that encourage reflection and discussion on the topic.

Please put the questions into a table"

EXAMPLE

"Create a survey for students to gather opinions and experiences about online learning from their fellow students.

The survey should include five questions of a variety of open-ended and multiple-choice questions that encourage reflection and discussion on the topic.

Please put the questions into a table"

TONGUE TWISTERS

PROMPT

"Create [number] tongue twisters for [student level] language students to practice their phonemic awareness and pronunciation of the sound [sound in IPA]

The tongue twisters should be funny and creative to inspire the students.

EXAMPLE

"Create five tongue twisters for beginner-level language students to practice their phonemic awareness and pronunciation of the sound /θ/.

The tongue twisters should be funny and creative to inspire the students."

TRUE OR FALSE

PROMPT

"Please generate a true-or-false quiz for language learners. The topic is [topic]. There should be [number] questions.

Please include these words or information to quiz on: [specific knowledge].

Please include an answer key."

EXAMPLE

"Please generate a multiple-choice quiz for language learners. The topic is history. There should be 10 questions.

Please include these words or information to quiz on:

The capital of the US; The US national bird; The shortest US presidency; The California gold rush.

Please include an answer key."

WORDSEARCH

PROMPT

"Please create a wordsearch puzzle for me in a codeblock. Underneath please tell me where the words are. Here are the words to use to create the puzzle: [10-15 words]."

Jaguar Leopard Sloth Chimpanzee Tiger Crocodile Elephant Gorilla Monkey Lion Tiger

EXAMPLE

"Please create a wordsearch puzzle for me in a codeblock. Underneath please tell me where the words are. Here are the words to use to create the puzzle:

Jaguar Leopard Sloth Chimpanzee Tiger Crocodile Elephant Gorilla Monkey Lion Tiger"

[Please note that this prompt only works in ChatGPT version 3]

IN THE CLASSROOM

GRADED LANGUAGE

PROMPT

"Please show how teachers can modify their instructions or explanations for beginner, intermediate, and advanced students.

Here are the instructions/explanations: [instructions or explanations]."

EXAMPLE

"Please show how teachers can modify an explanation for beginner, intermediate, and advanced students.

Here is the explanation:

The subjunctive isn't a tense. It's a mood. It's that wording you use when you talk about things you want or hope to happen. Unlike some other languages, English doesn't have a specific subjunctive verb form. Rather, phrases, clauses, and sentences express the subjunctive mood by using the bare form of a verb in a finite clause. Often, the verbs be or were are used as linking verbs in sentences written in the subjunctive mood.

CLASSROOM MANAGEMENT

PROMPT

"Please share strategies for language teachers to develop effective classroom management for [level] students who are [age range] years old.

Include tips on setting clear expectations, establishing routines, using positive reinforcement, and addressing behavioural issues."

EXAMPLE

"Please share strategies for language teachers to develop effective classroom management for beginner-level students who are 5-7 years old.

Include tips on setting clear expectations, establishing routines, using positive reinforcement, and addressing behavioural issues."

GIVING INSTRUCTIONS

PROMPT

"Please share strategies for language teachers to give instructions for [level] students who are [age range] years old.

Include tips on setting clear expectations and staging instructions, and questions to ask to ensure that students understand."

EXAMPLE

"Please share strategies for language teachers to give instructions for beginner-level students who are 7-10 years old.

Include tips on setting clear expectations and staging instructions, and questions to ask to ensure that students understand."

CONCEPT-CHECKING QUESTIONS

PROMPT

"Please share concept-checking questions that language teachers could ask their students to see if they've understand [language concept] being taught.

These questions are for [level] students who are [age range] years old."

EXAMPLE

"Please share concept-checking questions that language teachers could ask their students to see if they've understand the past progressive grammar tense being taught.

These questions are for intermediate students who are 13-15 years old."

ERRORS & FEEDBACK

PROMPT

"Please share strategies for language teachers to give effective feedback and positive reinforcement for [level] students who are [age range] years old.

Please include how and when to correct different types of errors they might make when learning about [language point]."

EXAMPLE

"Please share strategies for language teachers to give effective feedback and positive reinforcement for beginner students who are 5-7 years old.

Please include how and when to correct different types of errors they might make when learning about present simple tense."

ASSESSMENT & GRADING

FORMATIVE ASSESSMENT

PROMPT

"Please generate some ideas for formative assessments that I can use in my lesson on [language focus / topic] to check students are learning."

EXAMPLE

"Please generate some ideas for formative assessments that I can use in my lesson on present simple vs past simple to check students are learning."

"Please generate some ideas for formative assessments that I can use in my lesson on cultural differences between East and West to check students are learning."

STUDENT SELF-ASSESSMENT

PROMPT

"Please generate some ideas for student self-assessments that I can use in my lesson on [language focus / topic] to check students are learning."

EXAMPLE

"Please generate some ideas for student self-assessments that I can use in my lesson on present simple vs past simple to prompt students to reflect on their learning."

"Please generate some ideas for student self-assessments that I can use in my lesson on cultural differences between East and West to prompt students to reflect on their learning."

SUMMATIVE ASSESSMENT

PROMPT

"Please generate a quiz for this learning material [material].

Use the format [format].

Please include an answer key or suggested answers guide."

EXAMPLE

"Please generate a quiz for this learning material [unit syllabus pasted here].

Use the format of ten multiple choice questions with 4 possible answers each, and one short essay question (max 250 words).

Please include an answer key and/or suggested answers guide."

WRITTEN FEEDBACK

PROMPT

"Please write written feedback for this student work.

Give general feedback on [areas of interest], paying particular attention to [language focus].

Please write around [number] of words.

EXAMPLE

"Please write written feedback for this student work.

Give general feedback on vocabulary, grammar and style, paying particular attention to the present perfect tense.

Please write around 150 words.

CREATE A RUBRIC

PROMPT

"Please generate a rubric to help me assess this learning material [paste learning material].

Please put it in a table."

"Create a rubric for assessing students' written or oral work in a language class, focusing on the key aspects such as content, organization, grammar, vocabulary, and pronunciation.

Provide clear descriptions and criteria for each performance level, ranging from beginner to advanced, ensuring the rubric is easy to understand and apply for both teachers and students. Include any additional factors that might be important for evaluating language proficiency and growth."

GRADE WITH A RUBRIC

PROMPT

Act as a language teacher, analyze text and give supportive feedback based on a rubric that I will give you.

Students were given the following assignment:

[student assignment]

Here is the rubric:

[rubric]

Please give specific, constructive and meaningful feedback in a first-person, supportive voice, to a maximum [number] of words.

If the score given is less than [total points for the rubric] points, provide a brief paragraph on specific steps the student can do to improve the work and earn full credit based on the rubric.

PROFESSIONAL DEVELOPMENT

ASK QUESTIONS

PROMPT

[Any question you have about language teaching or learning!]

EXAMPLES

"What is 'extraneous cognitive load', and how does it relate to learning a language?"

"What is TBLT and how can I implement it into my language teaching?"

"How can I help students who are shy and don't want to speak in class?"

SUMMARIZING

PROMPT

"Here's some information I'd like to understand better:

[information pasted from the web or a pdf]

Please summarise this information and give me the key takeaways [in bullet points / in a short paragraph]. "

RESEARCH QUESTIONS

PROMPT

Please act as the author or researcher of this paper:

[paste research paper contents]

[Ask question you have about the paper]

ADMIN & DATA

ANALYSE DATA

PROMPT

"Here's a list of grades for [my student / my class] over the last [time period].

Please write a report for me using this data, highlighting any important data (high or low results) and the general overview of [the whole class / the student]

Please look at the results trend over time, if applicable. Please keep the report to a maximum of 500 words and use appropriate subheadings and bullet points."

EXAMPLES

"Here's a list of grades for my class over the last term.

Please write a report for me using this data, highlighting any important data (high or low results) and the general overview of the whole class.

Please look at the results trend over time, if applicable. Please keep the report to a maximum of 500 words and use appropriate subheadings and bullet points."

WRITE & SUMMARIZE EMAILS

PROMPT

"Please write an email to my Director of Studies and give him the results of the recent study [see last page].

Please give a summary in one paragraph."

"Here is a long email I received:

[paste email]

Please summarise it into a short paragraph or bullet points and give me any key actions I'm responsible for."

FINAL WORDS

THE FUTURE

If you'd like to share your prompts with me to include in the next version of the book (and will be credited to you!) then please send to me at:

david@barefootTEFLteacher.com

FREE NEWSLETTERS

I write two newsletters for teachers:

www.barefootTEFLteacher.com

Is for language teachers, and comes out twice a month.

www.AIEducatorNews.com

Is for all teachers interested in learning about AI and how to use it. It comes out every Friday.

Sign up and stay in touch for free.

OTHER BOOKS BY THE AUTHOR

You can find them all on Amazon at: https://geni.us/sslink

Printed in Great Britain
by Amazon

28135946R00040